Explore Space!

Mission Control

by Deborah A. Shearer

Consultant:
James Gerard
Aerospace Education Specialist
NASA Aerospace Education Services Program

Bridgestone Books
an imprint of Capstone Press
Mankato, Minnesota

Bridgestone Books are published by Capstone Press
151 Good Counsel Drive, P.O. Box 669, Mankato, Minnesota 56002
http://www.capstone-press.com

Library of Congress Cataloging-in-Publication Data
Shearer, Deborah A.
    Mission control / by Deborah A. Shearer.
    p. cm.—(Explore space!)
    Includes bibliographical references and index.
    Summary: Describes the role of NASA engineers, technicians, and other specialists
who stay on the ground in Houston, Texas, supporting astronauts as they journey on the
space shuttle.
    ISBN 0-7368-1143-5
    1. Ground support systems (Astronautics)—Juvenile literature. [1. Ground support
systems (Astronautics) 2. Space shuttles.] I. Title. II. Series.
TL4015 .S53 2002
629.47′8—dc21
        2001003505

Editorial Credits
Tom Adamson, editor; Karen Risch, product planning editor; Steve Christensen,
    cover designer; Linda Clavel, production designer and illustrator; Katy Kudela,
    photo researcher

Photo Credits
© Digital Vision, 12
NASA, cover, 4, 6, 8, 10, 14, 16, 18, 20

1 2 3 4 5 6 07 06 05 04 03 02

Table of Contents

Mission Control Center

Astronauts travel into space on space shuttles. Each shuttle trip has a mission. Flight controllers at Mission Control help astronauts complete their missions. Mission Control is at the Johnson Space Center in Houston, Texas.

space shuttle

a spacecraft that carries astronauts into space and back to Earth

5

FCR stands for Flight Control Room. People who work there call the FCR "Ficker."

Flight Control Room

Flight controllers watch spacecraft 24 hours per day. Many computers and screens fill the Flight Control Room. These screens show where the space shuttle is at all times. Flight controllers use computers to check on the astronauts and the shuttle.

Flight Control Jobs

Several teams of flight controllers work on every mission. The CAPCOM team talks to the astronauts. The Flight Dynamics Officer is called "Fido." Fido makes sure everything goes well on the shuttle during the mission. The flight director is in charge of the entire mission.

Kennedy Space Center

Launch Control at Kennedy Space Center in Florida tests and launches space shuttles. The first shuttle lifted off in 1981. Launch Control leads the countdown. It makes sure all computers needed to launch the shuttle are working.

countdown
counting backward down to zero; the shuttle rises off the ground when the countdown reaches zero.

Launch

Launch is the most dangerous 10 minutes of the flight. Rocket boosters give extra power to the shuttle. They are like giant fireworks that cannot be turned off. Launch Control handles a launch from liftoff until the shuttle clears the launch pad.

liftoff
the movement of a spacecraft as it rises off the ground

Johnson Space Center

Mission Control at Johnson Space Center takes over right after launch. The flight controllers check the engines, the shuttle's direction, and the amount of fuel. They watch for any changes in the life support systems.

fuel
something that is burned for power

15

Landing

Mission Control talks with the astronauts during landing. The shuttle usually lands at Kennedy Space Center. If the weather is stormy in Florida, the shuttle lands at Edwards Air Force Base in California. The shuttle lands like a glider. A parachute opens to help it stop.

glider
a winged aircraft that floats on air currents instead of using engine power

17

Space Station

Mission Control also keeps track of the space station. Astronauts live there and need help from Mission Control. The Marshall Center in Alabama checks the science experiments on the space station. Astronauts do experiments to learn how people adapt to being in space.

experiment
a scientific test to learn something new

The Future

Mission Control will be important to astronauts and spacecraft in the future. Astronauts will go on longer space missions. They will stay on the space station for months at a time. Mission Control will guide astronauts as they spend more time in space.

Hands On: Be a Fight Controller

Mission Control has to communicate with astronauts over great distances. Mission Control helps astronauts get tasks done. With a friend, you can pretend to talk to an astronaut on a space mission.

What You Need

Doorway with closed door
Pencil and paper
Building materials such as blocks

What You Do

1. One person is a flight controller and gives directions. One person is the astronaut in space and follows directions.
2. Each person stands on each side of a closed door.
3. The flight controller gives directions to the astronaut. The directions could be to place one block on top of another, or to draw a picture of something.
4. The flight controller should keep track of each instruction he or she gives the astronaut. Write down each step.
5. The astronaut should listen carefully and follow the steps.
6. After you are finished, the flight controller can look at what the astronaut did. Did the flight controller give good directions? Did the astronaut follow directions well?
7. Change places and try again.

Words to Know

astronaut (ASS-truh-nawt)—a person who is trained to live and work in space

booster (BOO-stur)—a rocket that gives extra power to a spacecraft

CAPCOM (KAP-kom)—short for Capsule Communication; astronauts make up this team of flight controllers.

engine (EN-juhn)—a machine that makes the power needed to move something

launch (LAWNCH)—to send a space shuttle into space

mission (MISH-uhn)—an important job or task

parachute (PA-ruh-shoot)—a large piece of strong, lightweight cloth that helps the shuttle slow down after it lands

Read More

Atkinson, Stuart. *Space Travel*. Space Busters. Austin, Texas: Raintree Steck-Vaughn, 2002.

Bredeson, Carmen. *Our Space Program*. I Know America. Brookfield, Conn.: Millbrook Press, 1999.

Vogt, Gregory L. *Space Shuttles*. Explore Space! Mankato, Minn.: Bridgestone Books, 1999.

Internet Sites

Canadian Space Agency—KidSpace
http://www.space.gc.ca/kidspace/default.asp
Space & Beyond
http://kids.msfc.nasa.gov/Space

Index